THE BEST OF
CANADA

EXPLORAMA

A CONTEMPLATIVE JOURNEY TO CANADA

Toronto

Toronto

Toronto

Toronto

Toronto

Niagara Falls

Niagara Falls

London

Windsor

Owen Sound

Bruce Peninsula

Algonquin Provincial Park

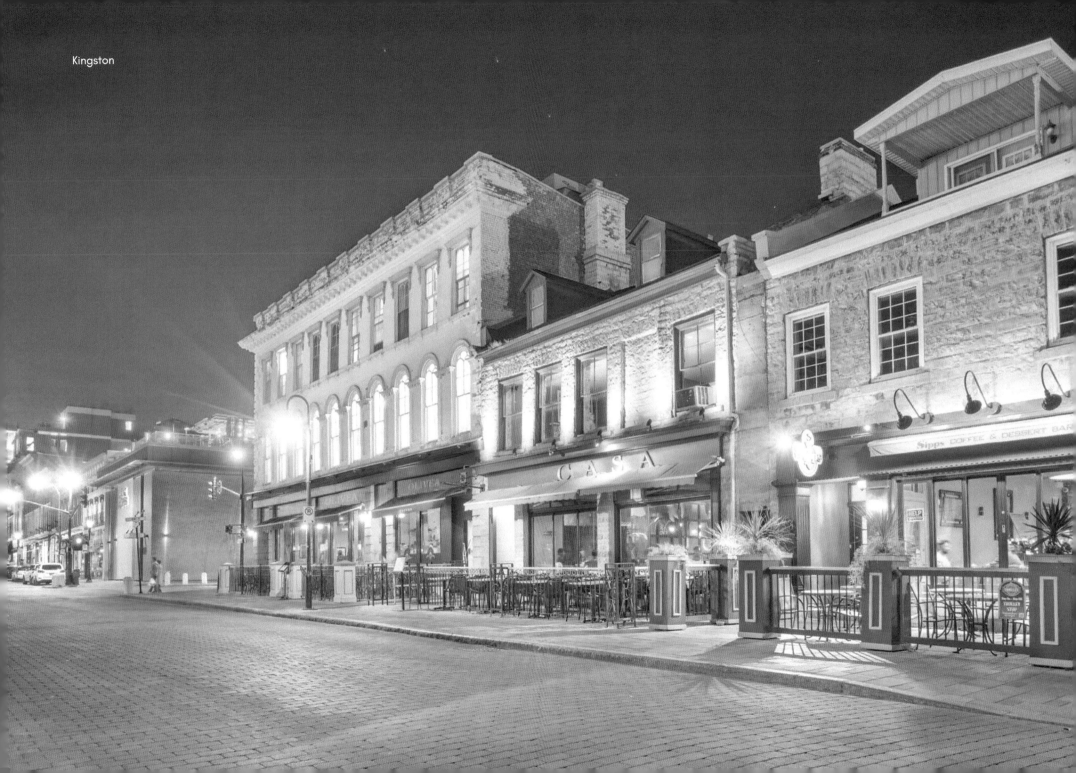

Kingston

Brockville

Ottawa

Ottawa

Ottawa

Thunder Bay

Montréal

Montréal

Montréal

Montréal

Montréal

Mont-Tremblant

Magog

Sherbrooke

Trois-Rivières

Québec City

Québec City

Québec City

Québec City

Île d'Orléans

Parc national de la Jacques-Cartier

Gaspé Peninsula – Percé

Baie-Saint-Paul

Parc national du Bic

Tadoussac

Les Escoumins

Fjord du Saguenay

Chicoutimi

Lac Saint-Jean

Archipel-de-Mingan

Halifax

Halifax

Lunenburg

Digby

Annapolis Royal

Cape Blomidon

Cape Breton Island

Chéticamp

Meat Cove

Louisbourg

Alma

Fundy National Park

Saint John

Saint John

Campobello Island

Fredericton

Dune de Bouctouche

Charlottetown

French River

Prince Edward Island (Westpoint)

Malpeque Harbour

St John's

St John's

Cape Spear National Historic Site

Ferryland

Brigus

Cape Bonavista

Terra Nova National Park

Fogo Island

Twillingate

Gros Morne National Park

Norris Point

Winnipeg

Winnipeg

Winnipeg

Riding Mountain National Park

Saskatoon

Saskatoon

Elk Island National Park

Edmonton

Edmonton

Edmonton

Qu'Appelle River Valley

Regina

Regina

Big Muddy Valley

Grasslands National Park

Great Sand Hills

Medicine Hat

Dinosaur Provincial Park

Calgary

Calgary

Calgary

Calgary

Calgary

Calgary

Canmore

Kananaskis Valley

Banff

Banff National Park

Banff National Park

Sunshine Meadows

Icefields Parkway

Jasper national park

Mount Robson Provincial Park

Lake O'Hara

Crowsnest Pass

Osoyoos

Osoyoos

Kelowna

Kelowna

Vernon

Shuswap Lake

Kamloops

Wells Gray Provincial Park

Vancouver

Vancouver

Vancouver

Vancouver

Vancouver

Vancouver

Vancouver

Vancouver

Vancouver

Vancouver

Sea to Sky Highway

Sea to Sky Highway

Whistler

Barkerville

Victoria

Victoria

Victoria

Port Renfrew

Nanaimo

Pacific Rim National Park

Bamfield

Bamfield

Strathcona Provincial Park

Haida Gwaii

Haida Gwaii

Bear Glacier

Whitehorse

Kluane National Park

Dawson City

Dempster Highway

Yellowknife

Yellowknife

Yellowknife

Nunavut

Baffin Island

Iqaluit

Canada

A contemplative journey through some of the most beautiful places.

Explorama

Nunavut

Nunavut